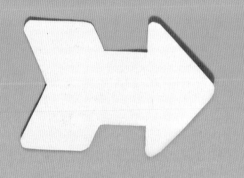

First U.S. edition 2020

First edition published by Pequeño
Editor (Argentina) and Oceano
(Mexico) 2009

Second edition published by Pequeño
Editor (Argentina) 2015

Library of Congress Catalog
Card Number pending

ISBN 978-1-5362-0021-8

25 24 23 22 21 20
TLF 10 9 8 7 6 5 4 3 2 1

Dongguan, Guangdong, China

This book was typeset in Helvetica
Neue and Lucky Flamingo.

Candlewick Press
99 Dover Street
Somerville, Massachusetts 02144

visit us at www.candlewick.com

Thanks to Eduardo Carletti and his well-trained ants; to architects POLI + BOXACA, for hauling the sugarcane all the
way from Tucumán; to Adriana and her family of Saint Bernards; to Tofi, the cow from Chocolate Farm; to Noemí
Bialostocky, of Vassallo Pharmacy, who helped us calculate how much a single grain of sand weighs; to Alberto Kreindel,
of Llerena Textile, who told us how to unravel a T-shirt; to J.L., of Vicente López, the last of the old-school watchmakers;
to the elephant and the camel from the Luján Zoo; to Gabriel, the balloon man; to Esteban, the gardener, who lent us
his archenemies, the snails, for the photo; to Pedro Katzeinstein, Juan Cottet, and Pedro Doneiger, the child models; to
Tania Domenicucci, who kicked off the research; to Vero Colombo, for her magical scissors . . .

and, most especially, to my family:
Caro, Felipe, and Pedro.

CURIOUS COMPARISONS

A Life-Size Look at the World Around You

JORGE DONEIGER

photographs by GUIDO CHOUELA, CRISTINA RECHE, MARCELO SETTON, AND DAVID SISSO

translated from the Spanish by IRAIDA ITURRALDE

CANDLEWICK PRESS

Everything you will see in these pages is shown at its real-life size:

it's a life-size book.

THE SNAIL'S PATH

**When a snail is hungry,
it has no choice but
to get going.**

**It took this snail 2 minutes to travel
10 inches (25 centimeters).**

WHEN A SNAIL
GETS SLEEPY,
IT DOESN'T HAVE TO WORRY.
ITS HOUSE
TRAVELS
WITH IT
WHEREVER IT GOES.

A long, long time passed between the invention of the windup clock . . . and the invention of the battery-operated alarm clock that wakes us up each morning.

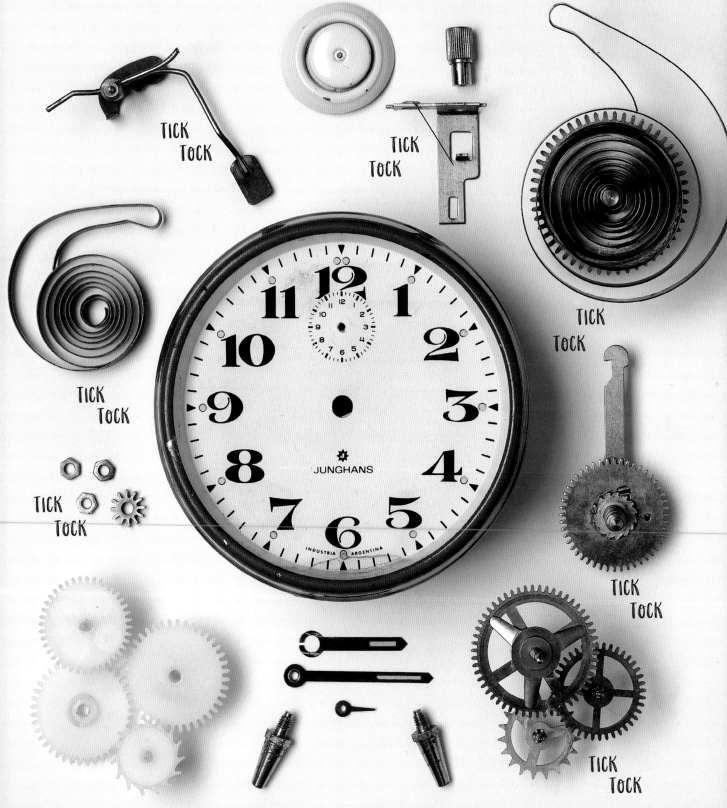

TICK TOCK

TICK TOCK

TICK TOCK

TICK TOCK

TICK TOCK

TICK TOCK

TICK TOCK

TICK TOCK

JUNGHANS

INDUSTRIA ARGENTINA

BEEP
BEEEEEEP
BEEP
BEEEEEEP

THERE IS ANOTHER WAY
TO MEASURE THE PASSAGE OF TIME:
IN THE CHANGES WE SEE IN THE THINGS AROUND US
AND IN OURSELVES.

In a single bucket you can find around 120 million grains of sand.

THAT'S MORE THAN ALL THE PEOPLE WHO LIVE IN ARGENTINA, CHILE, URUGUAY, PARAGUAY, BOLIVIA, AND PERU COMBINED.

BITS OF PEBBLES AND SHELLS
HIDE IN
THE SAND
AND MAY SURPRISE YOU.

The tip of a pencil can create
ships, airplanes, and monsters,
but it can also make crazy scribbles.

How much can a pencil draw?

BEFORE MAKING THIS SCRIBBLE,
THIS PENCIL MEASURED
AROUND 6½ INCHES (17 CENTIMETERS) LONG.

SHARPENING
A PENCIL
MIGHT BE BORING,
BUT SCRIBBLING
IS
SUPER FUN.

We all enjoy a picnic with friends, and so do these guys. . . .

It would take around 50 ants to steal a piece of cake.

SOME ANTS CAN CARRY LOADS 100 TIMES HEAVIER THAN THEIR OWN WEIGHT.

SET ANOTHER PLATE.
WE HAVE
COMPANY!

**The ostrich
is the largest
bird in the
world.**

A SINGLE OSTRICH EGG IS EQUIVALENT IN VOLUME TO 24 CHICKEN EGGS.

THAT WOULD MAKE ONE **DELICIOUS** AND **GIGANTIC** FRIED EGG!

YOU'LL NEED
SOME FRIENDS
TO HELP YOU
EAT IT.

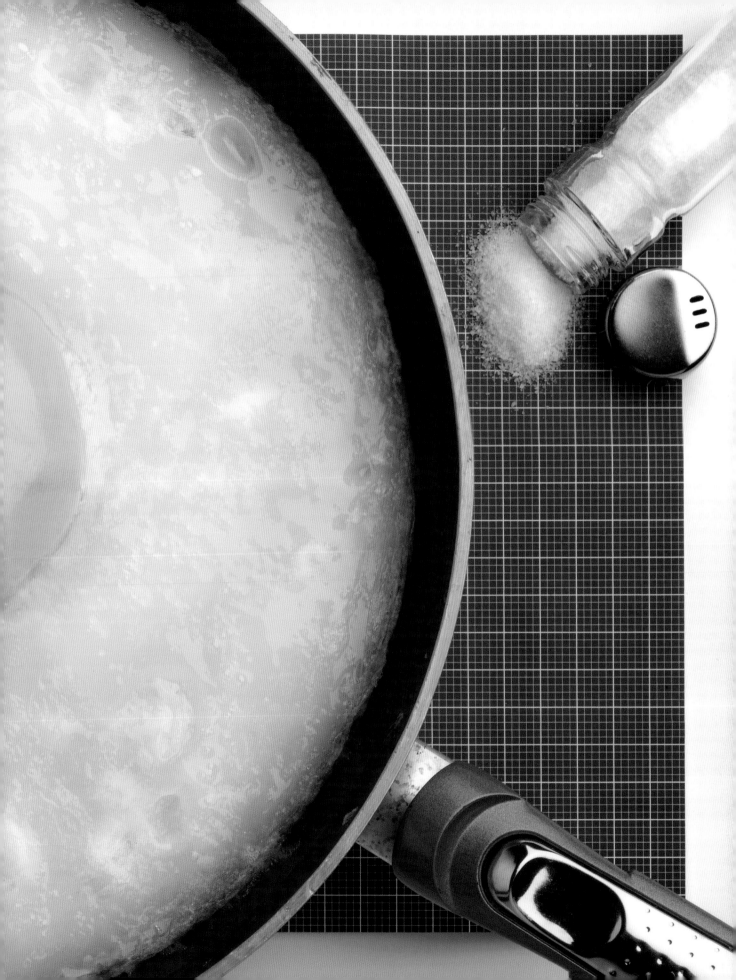

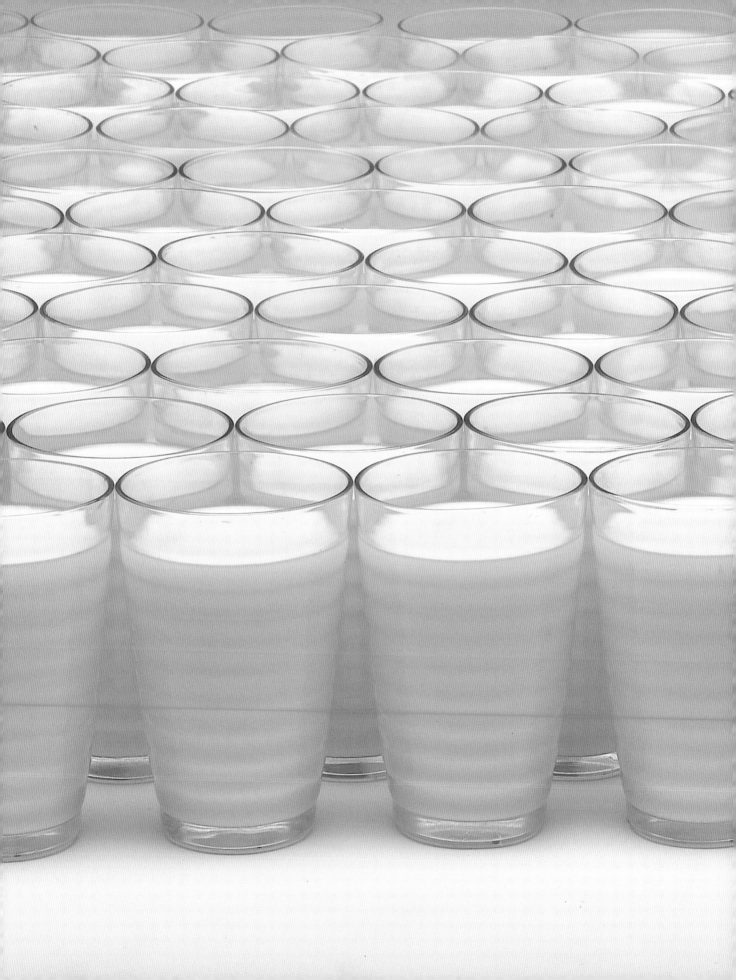

THE EXTRA MILK COULD FILL AROUND 95 GLASSES!

One cow can produce around 7 gallons (27 liters) of milk a day.

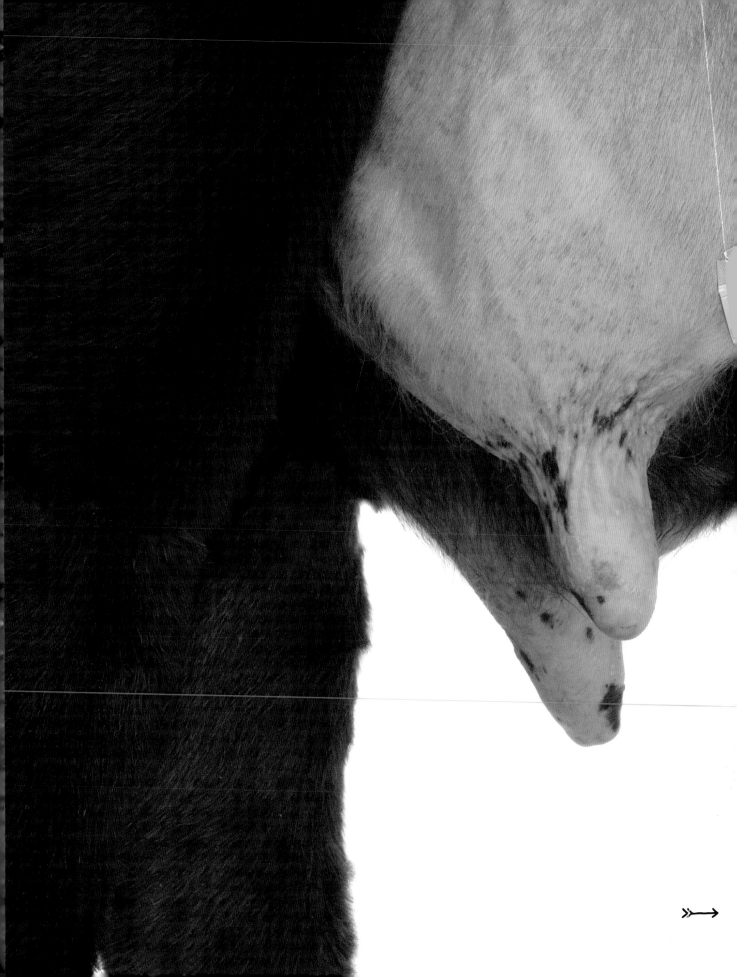

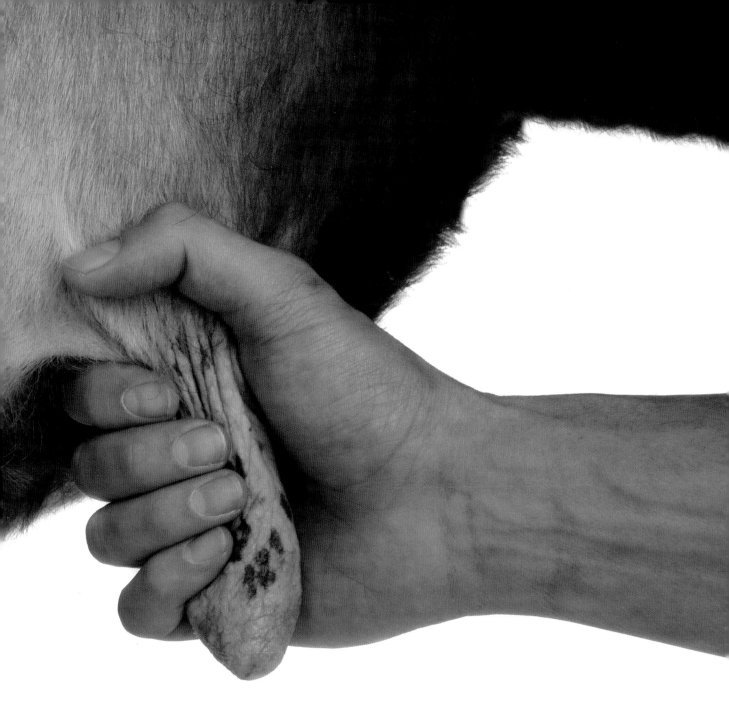

When a cow gives birth, she produces more milk than her calf needs.

More than you can imagine!

←—«

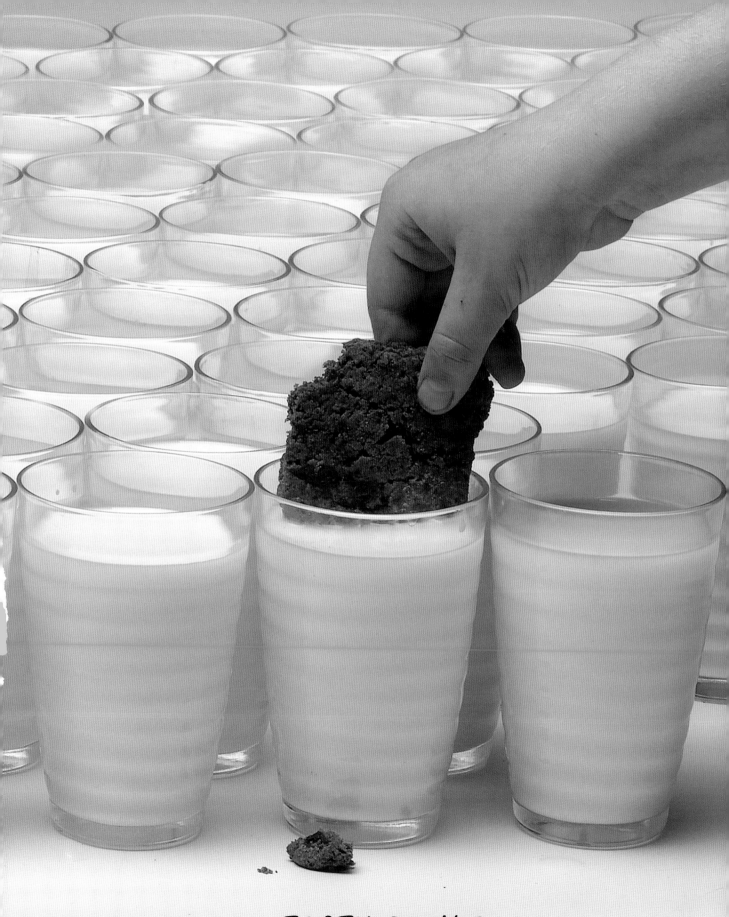

THESE, I HOPE YOU ALWAYS HAVE A **TASTY COOKIE.**

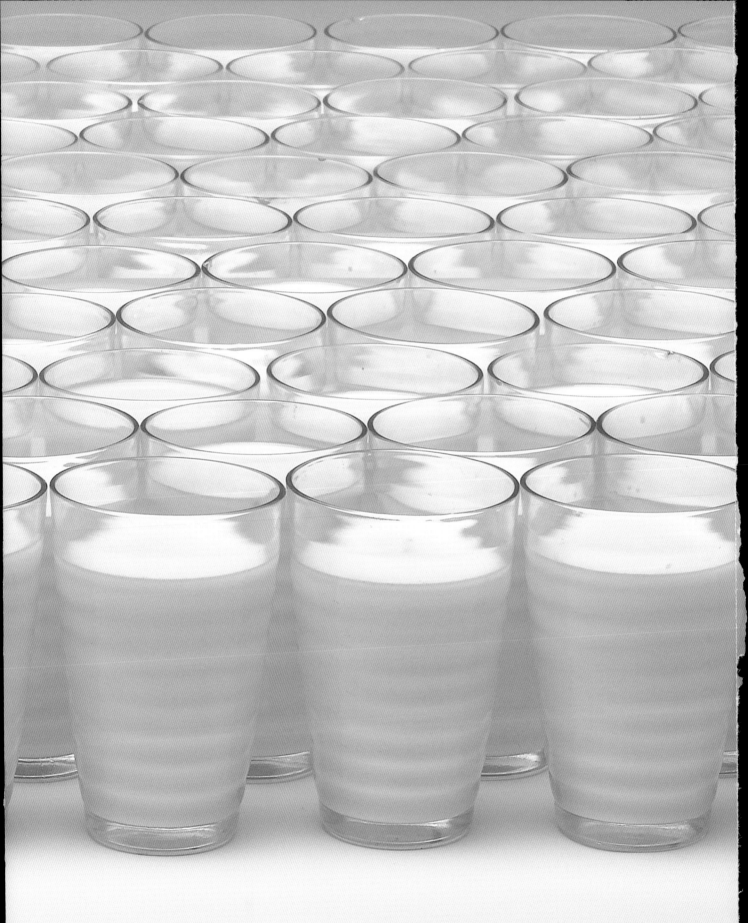

AT TIMES LIKE

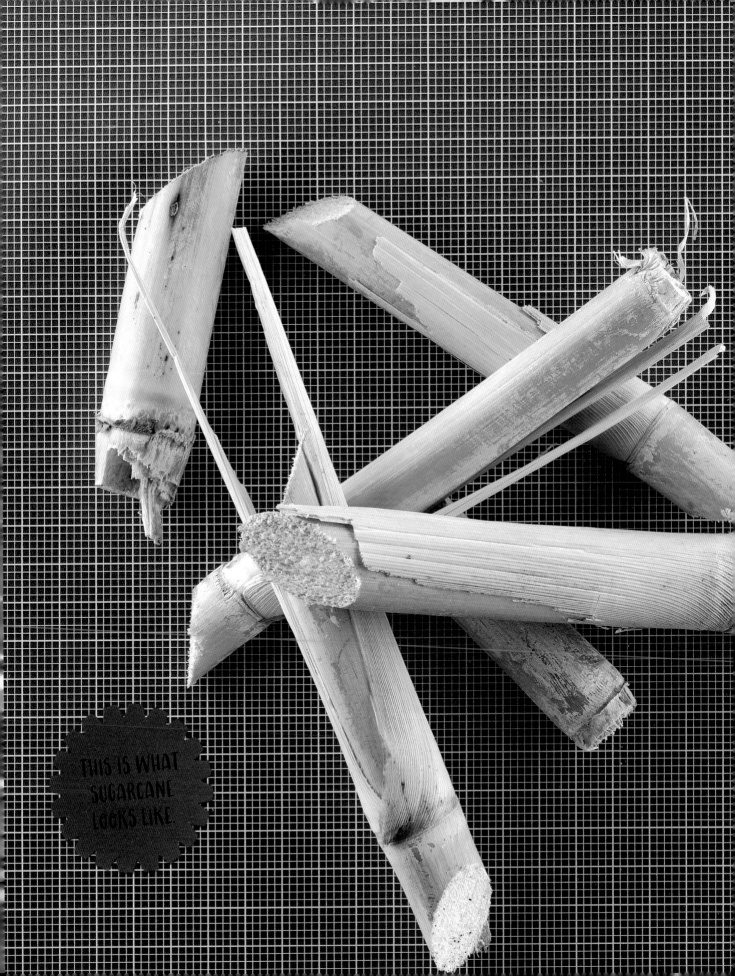

THIS IS WHAT
SUGARCANE
LOOKS LIKE

You need around 5¼ ounces (150 grams) of sugarcane to make a single piece of candy.

THERE'S NOTHING
YUMMIER
THAN A
DELICIOUS
PIECE OF CANDY.

**Which weighs more:
a pound of feathers or
a pound of lead?**

IT SEEMS LIKE AN EASY QUESTION. BUT CAN YOU IMAGINE

HOW HARD IT WOULD BE TO FLY WITH LEAD FEATHERS?

This is the boot that took Neil Armstrong to the moon.

Your shoes can take you anywhere you can imagine.

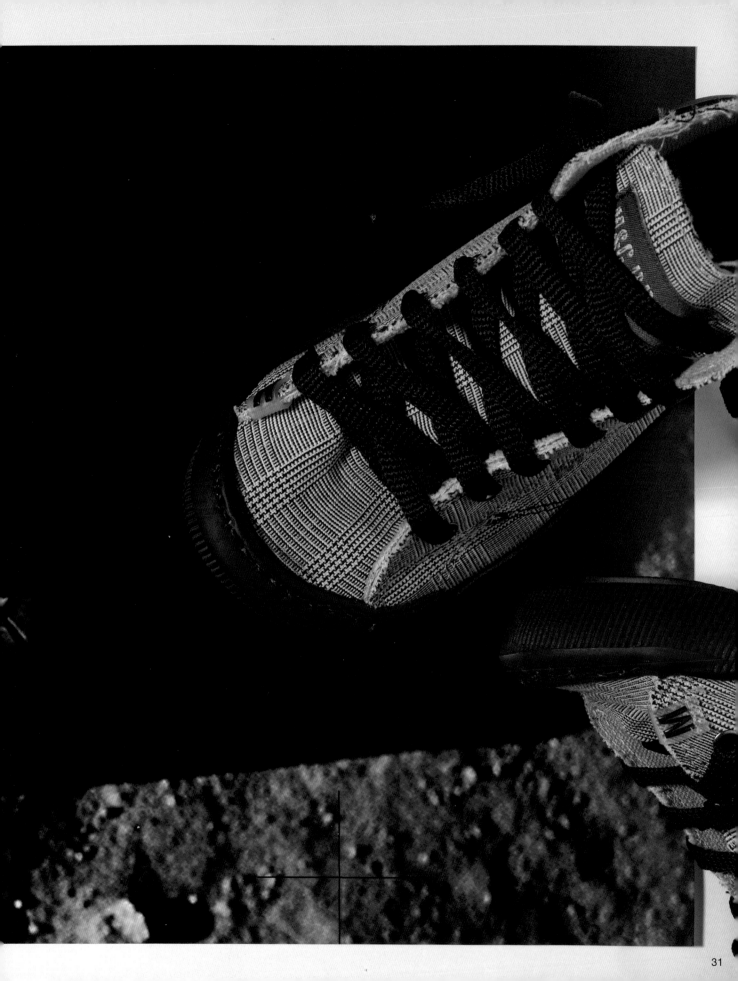

When a camel is thirsty, there's no stopping him.
He can drink more than 30 gallons (114 liters) of water in one fell swoop.

COULD THIS BE WHY THERE'S
SO LITTLE WATER
LEFT IN THE DESERT?

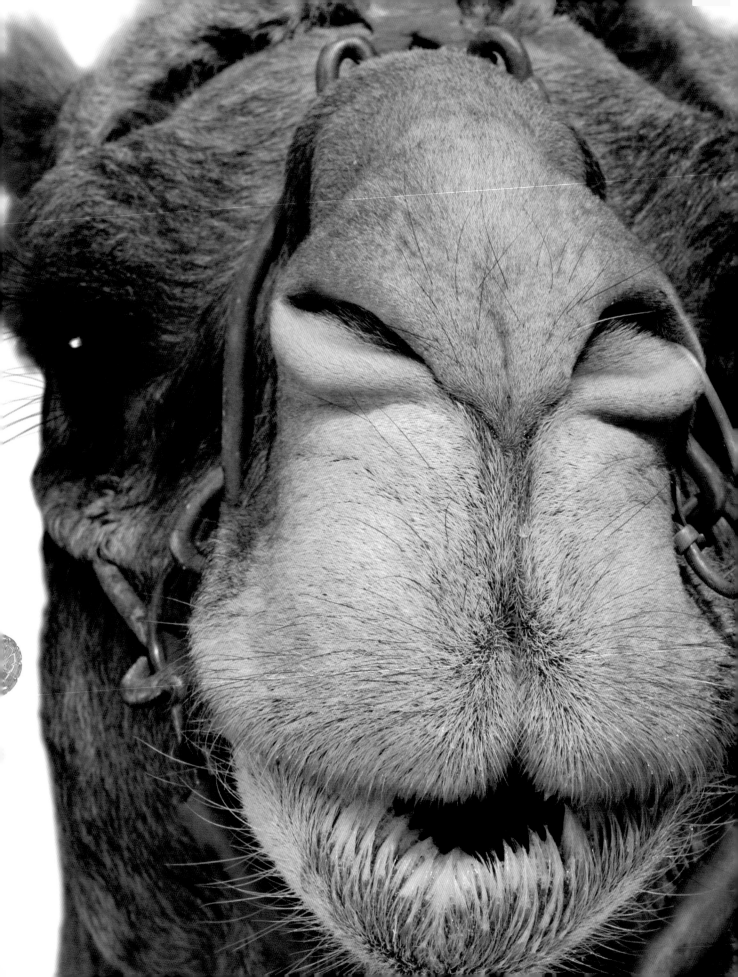

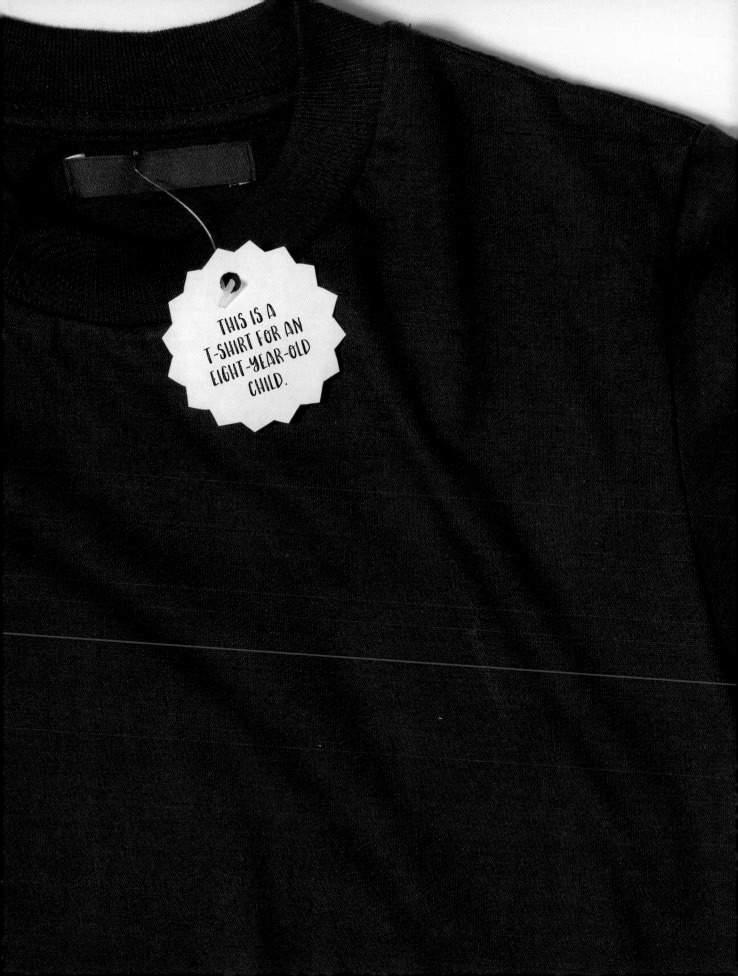

THIS IS A
T-SHIRT FOR AN
EIGHT-YEAR-OLD
CHILD.

What if we
pull and pull
and the thread
doesn't break?
What if we
unravel it all?

»——→

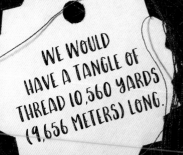

The thread it takes to make a single T-shirt could wrap around a city block about 14 times.

WE WOULD HAVE A TANGLE OF THREAD 10,560 YARDS (9,656 METERS) LONG.

THERE'S NOTHING MORE TEMPTING
THAN A LOOSE THREAD
DANGLING FROM A T-SHIRT!

Three ears of corn will more than fill a large bag of popcorn.

IT IS HARD TO IMAGINE THAT THESE EARS OF CORN COULD TURN INTO

IT TOOK 4 OUNCES (115 GRAMS) OF POPPED KERNELS TO FILL THIS BAG.

ONE OF THE **TASTIEST SNACKS** TO EAT WHILE WATCHING A GOOD MOVIE.

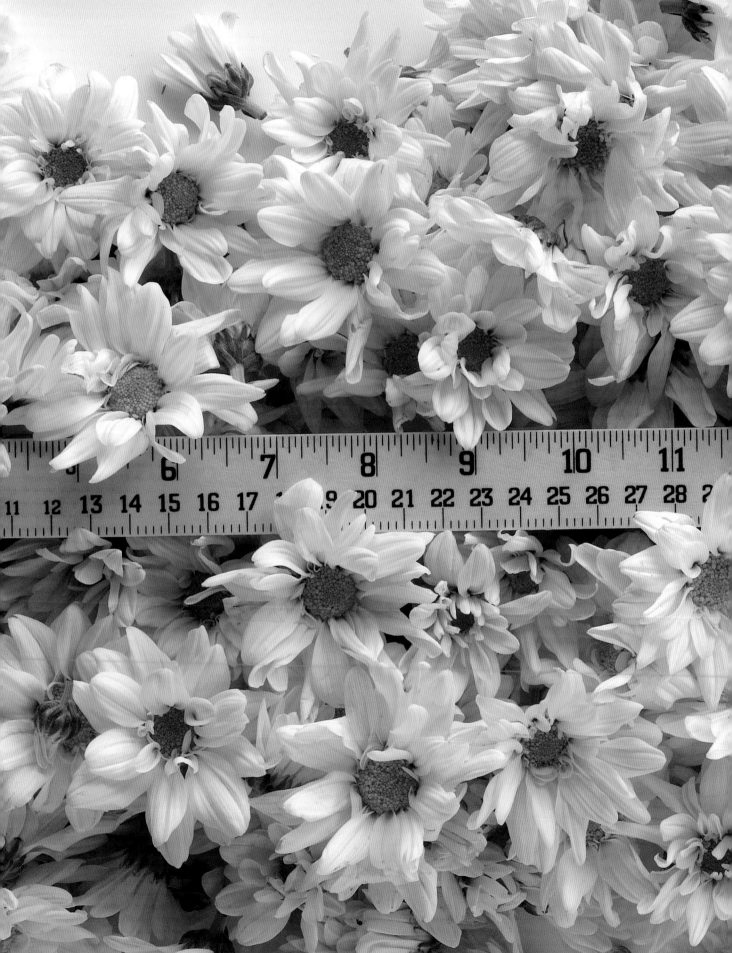

To make a pound of honey, a hive of bees needs to collect pollen from about 2 million flowers.

The worker bee spends her whole adult life looking for flowers to make her food: honey.

»→

HOW MUCH WORK
WILL IT TAKE THE BEE
AND HER HIVE MATES
TO MAKE A
SINGLE POUND
OF HONEY?

←«

COULD THE LIFE
OF A BEE BE AS
SWEET AS IT SEEMS?

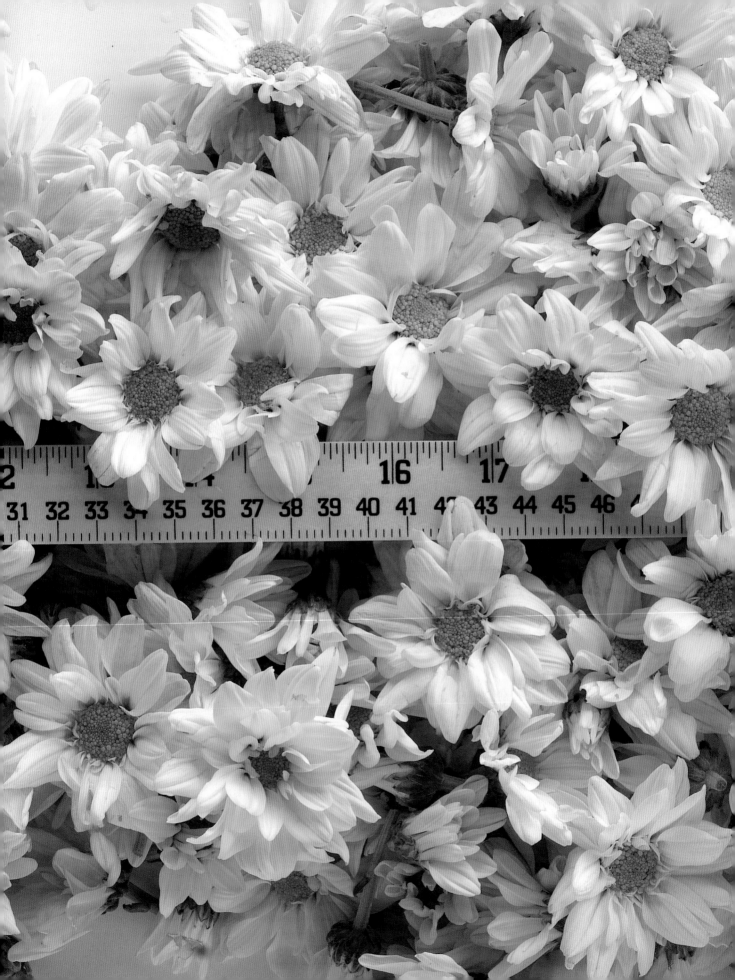

While we play, while we eat,
while we sleep . . . we breathe.

If we could collect all the air
we breathe in a single day,
we could fill more than 800 balloons.

IT'S GOOD TO HAVE FRESH AIR TO BREATHE.

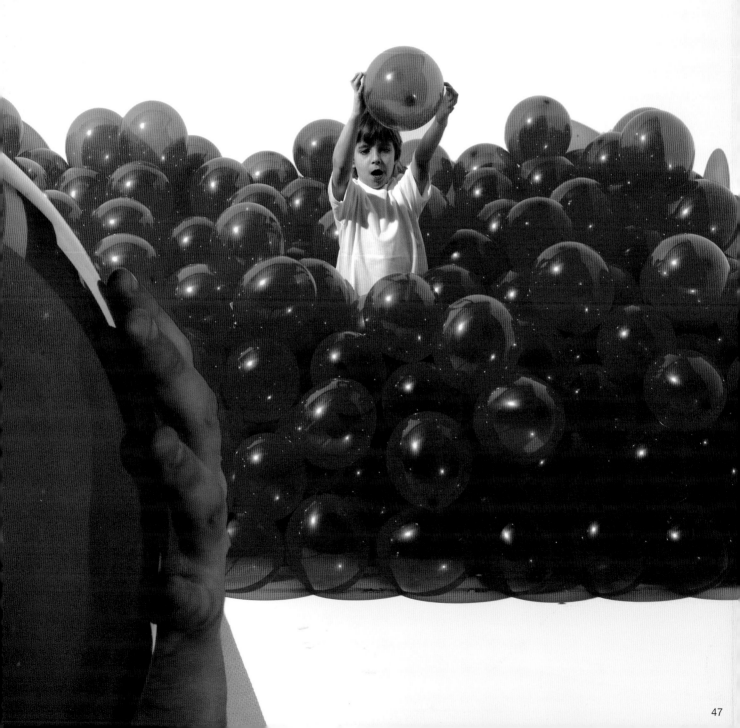

When the first leaves appear, we know that spring has arrived.

In the summer, we cool off under their shade.

IN JUST 10 MONTHS, THE LEAVES SPROUT, GROW, AND CHANGE COLOR.

In the fall
everything
changes . . .
different smells,
different colors.

In the winter,
the tree rests and
gathers strength
to begin again.

TIME CAN BE MEASURED IN COLORS.

They say that a single mouse can scare a whole herd of elephants.

AND THE LITTLE MOUSE JUST WANTED TO

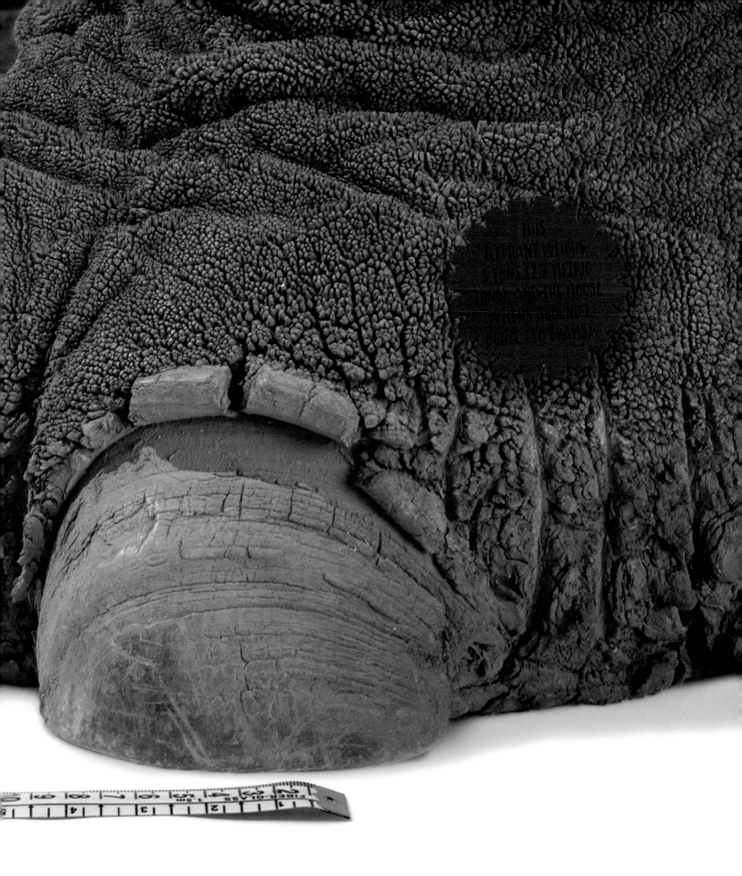

THIS ELEPHANT WEIGHS 6 TONS (2.7 TONNE) AND THE HOUSE WEIGHS 94 TONS (100 METRIC TONS)

MAKE A **NEW FRIEND.**

Inside this pod you can find around 30 to 40 cacao seeds.

After you dry and grind them, and mix them with milk and sugar . . .

THIS IS A CACAO POD FROM BRAZIL.

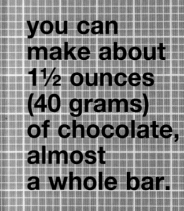

you can
make about
1½ ounces
(40 grams)
of chocolate,
almost
a whole bar.

WHAT WOULD

LIFE BE LIKE

WITHOUT

CHOCOLATE?

Attila is a two-year-old Saint Bernard who weighs around 198 pounds (90 kilograms).

He needs a lot of food to keep up his energy for playing, running, and jumping.

LIKE ALL DOGS, HE WILL WANT TO EAT WHATEVER HE FINDS, BUT HE SHOULD ONLY EAT AROUND 2 POUNDS (1 KILOGRAM) OF DOG FOOD PER DAY.

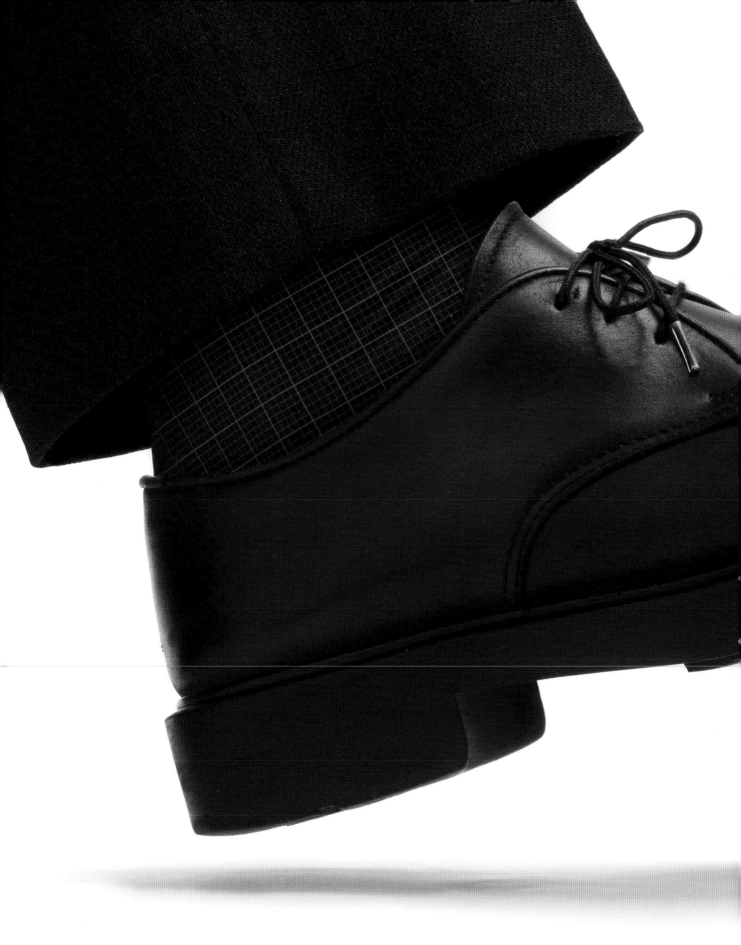

Joseph is Attila's owner, and he's about to get a surprise gift from his cute doggie. . . .

This is the amount
of wood you need
to make the paper
for a book
like the one
you're holding.

THE PAPER FOR THIS
BOOK WAS MADE FROM
TREES PROTECTED
BY RESPONSIBLE
FOREST MANAGEMENT.

THIS PIECE OF WOOD
WEIGHS AROUND 2 POUNDS
(950 GRAMS).
AND THIS BOOK WEIGHS
AROUND 1 POUND
(450 GRAMS).

Life-Size Facts for the Very Curious

SPEED DEMONS

A snail on the move leaves a trail of slime behind it. That slime is a thick liquid that allows the snail to drag itself along the ground without getting scraped.

The snail is a slow-moving creature: some can travel only 15 feet (4.5 meters) in an hour. But there are others who are speed demons (in snail terms, of course) and can travel up to 150 feet (45 meters) in that time.

There are thousands of species of land snails, and they all move by curling up and stretching out their bodies. They are called gastropods, which means "stomach foot" — fitting for a creature that crawls on its belly.

MEASURING TIME

Humans spent hundreds of years trying to build a clock that could accurately measure time. They used sundials, water clocks, and hourglasses filled with sand, but none of them were reliable, and not one of them gave the same time as the other.

This was a problem until the invention of mechanical clocks in the thirteenth or fourteenth century. Since then it's been much easier to arrange a meeting! Today there are world clocks that coordinate time over the Internet.

And we each have our own unique clock from the moment we are born: a biological clock. This internal clock regulates our basic needs. It tells us when it's time to eat or sleep, for example. That's why people who travel to faraway places might change time zones but feel like their body is still on the same schedule as the place they left. So a person might be tired during the day, feel alert at night, and get hungry at the strangest times. Our biological clocks don't care what time it is on the clocks around the world.

IT WOULD TAKE YOU TWENTY-FOUR HOURS TO GET TO THE OTHER SIDE OF THE WORLD BY PLANE.

BUT IT CAN TAKE YOUR BODY SEVEN DAYS OR MORE TO ADJUST TO THE TIME DIFFERENCE.

SAND: FRAGMENTS OF EVERYTHING

The sand you see on our planet's beaches was formed by many different substances that have accumulated over millions of years. These substances include fragments of rocks that the ocean has washed up, sediment from the bottom of rivers, pieces of mountains blown away by the wind, ashes from volcanoes, bits of shells, and even fish waste.

Sand helps us understand that some gigantic things are made up of many small things: the vast Sahara desert is a collection of countless little grains of sand.

FROM GRAPHITE TO DIAMOND

Graphite, the material that makes our pencils write, is formed by carbon atoms. Just like diamonds! Graphite and diamonds are made from the same chemical element, even though they don't look anything alike.

ANTS AT A PICNIC

Biologists say that ants are resilient insects, since they can live almost anywhere in the world (even in the Arctic and in deserts). Of course, there are many different kinds of ants with different behaviors and ways of getting nourishment. They wouldn't all steal a slice of cake from your picnic blanket!

One unusual type of ant herds aphids (plant lice). Since ants and aphids like the same plants, the ants let the aphids do all the work of sucking up the sap, and then they milk them! In return for this service, the ants protect the aphids: they lead them to fresh leaves, they cover them if it rains, and they drive away other insects that might attack them.

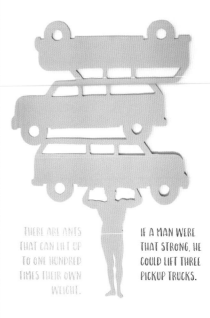

THERE ARE ANTS THAT CAN LIFT UP TO ONE HUNDRED TIMES THEIR OWN WEIGHT.

IF A MAN WERE THAT STRONG, HE COULD LIFT THREE PICKUP TRUCKS.

THE BIRD THAT FORGOT HOW TO FLY

Some scholars say that ostriches could fly thousands of years ago. But since they lived in environments with abundant food and without enemies to chase them, they started growing, gaining weight and getting taller, until one day they were too big to take off and fly.

Today's ostriches can only run, but they run very fast, reaching speeds of 45 miles (70 kilometers) per hour. They have the help of their long legs and strong feet that grip the ground. Ostriches once lived in Asia, the Arabian Peninsula, and Africa, but because of overhunting, the wild ostrich population is declining and is now found only in sub-Saharan Africa.

THE SACRED COW

Humans are omnivorous; that means that we can eat all kinds of food. Our ability to nourish ourselves with many kinds of plants and animals has helped our species to survive and multiply.

However, every culture or region has different tastes. In some cultures, people eat ants or beetles, while in other cultures insects would never be on the menu. There are also some foods that are forbidden in certain cultures. In many places around the world, meat from a cow is considered a delicacy; in India, however, eating beef is taboo. There, a majority of the population practices Hinduism, and the cow is considered a sacred symbol. Luckily for cows, there are around one billion people who follow this religion.

CANDY HARVEST

Most people believe that candy is just a treat and doesn't have much nutritional value. But candy was created to relieve our hunger and give us a quick boost of energy, all in one bite. It's long been part of human culture. That's why it has played a role in some important historical events. Need an example? In 1948, after World War II, Germany was controlled by multiple countries. But the Soviet Union wanted to be the only country to rule Germany, so it cut off all the roads that went to the capital, Berlin. As a result, the people who lived in that city could not get food. The other countries came up with a clever plan to help them: for more than a year they sent airplanes to fly over Berlin and drop food, coal, and medicine. They also dropped candies and lollipops. The kids who lived in the city would chase after the planes so they could be the first to get the packages of candy.

THE WEIGHT OF THINGS

A pound of feathers weighs exactly the same as a pound of lead, although it might not seem like it at first glance. Both have the same amount of matter: one pound. How can that be? They are two different substances: just a small amount of lead weighs one pound, while it takes many, many feathers to weigh one pound.

THE MOON'S SKY

On July 20, 1969, Neil Armstrong became the first man to walk on the moon. We already knew a lot about Earth's satellite, but on that day Armstrong confirmed some fundamental facts firsthand. To start with, the moon has very little atmosphere, and it doesn't contain the oxygen we need to breathe. Because there is almost no air, sound is not transmitted. The silence is deep and absolute. If we were on the surface of the moon and a rock band was playing right next to us, we wouldn't hear a thing.

Also, the moon doesn't have gases that protect it from solar radiation, so its surface can reach 260 degrees Fahrenheit (127 degrees Celsius). The sun's light is incredibly powerful. Yet on the moon, the sky is always black.

LIVING IN THE DESERT

On some parts of planet Earth, life is very harsh. In many areas, the weather is so extreme that only a few species are able to survive. In the terribly dry desert, it's burning hot during the day and freezing cold at night with little, if any, vegetation. Camels are very well adapted to these conditions. Their humps are actually large reserves of fat. They can go a long time without eating or eating very little. Plus, camels hardly sweat. Their bodies can endure very intense heat before starting to sweat, so they lose very little water. Camels have a body temperature that's lower than the air temperature. When they rest in the desert, they squeeze their bodies against each other to cool off. That's something no human would think of doing when it's 113° Fahrenheit (45° Celsius)!

THE HUMP OF A CAMEL IS LIKE A BIG BACKPACK FILLED WITH FOOD RESERVES.

IT'S A PILE OF FAT FROM WHICH A CAMEL EXTRACTS ENERGY WHEN FOOD IS HARD TO FIND.

THE CLOTHING PLANT

Cotton is a plant that is grown almost everywhere in the world. Its bud is so white and soft that some say that snowflakes are like little bits of cotton. Many products are made of cotton, from fuel to paper money. But cotton is really popular because it is also used to make jeans, T-shirts, and many of the clothes we wear.

Cotton can also be grown in different colors. The colored cotton typically doesn't grow as well as white cotton, but clothes made out of colored cotton don't have to be dyed.

THE PEOPLE OF CORN

Before the Spanish arrived in the Americas, they didn't know about corn. Corn was very important for the peoples of the region. For the ancient Mayans, corn was so special that it also played a role in their religion. According to Mayan legend, the first time the gods created man, they made him out of clay. But he turned out weak and unable to speak. Then the gods tried to make man out of sticks. But that didn't work out either. One day the gods discovered corn. They thought this grain was so exceptional that they used it to create man and woman. And those beings of corn turned out to be wise, hardworking, able to speak, and, of course, great farmers.

HONEY WORKERS

The life of a worker bee is exhausting. There can be up to 60,000 worker bees in a single hive, and their whole life revolves around work. In their first days of life, the worker bees do the "domestic" chores of the hive, such as caring for the eggs and larvae, cleaning and cooling the hive, and building the honeycomb cells. They don't work outside the hive until they become "adults." This happens when they turn twenty-one days old. They then leave the hive and handle all the fieldwork: they explore, collect water, gather nectar and pollen, and take it back to the hive. A worker bee lives between forty and forty-five days and then dies—often outside the hive.

THE BEES PERFORM A DANCE THAT THEY REPEAT SEVERAL TIMES TO INFORM THE REST OF THE BEES IN THE HIVE HOW FAR AND IN WHICH DIRECTION AN IMPORTANT SOURCE OF FOOD CAN BE FOUND.

THE WAGGLE DANCE INDICATES THE FOOD SOURCE IS FARTHER AWAY.

THE ROUND DANCE INDICATES THE FOOD SOURCE IS CLOSE.

A VERY UNUSUAL PLANET

We need oxygen to live, but oxygen is scarce in the universe. On some planets there is very little of it, and on others there may be none at all. More than 2 billion years ago, there wasn't any oxygen on Earth either. None whatsoever. But at some point in time (as recently as 3.5 billion years ago), water appeared. And in that water bluish-green bacteria emerged. These bacteria did something special: they took in hydrogen from the water and released oxygen!

The bacteria multiplied to such an extent that our atmosphere filled with oxygen. This was a momentous change that allowed new types of organisms to emerge, including those that give off oxygen (plants) and those that take it in (animals).

Today, nearly all life on our planet, including human life, revolves around oxygen.

LEAVES, THE GREAT PLANNERS

Leaves take care of feeding the planet. They capture sunlight and use it to turn water, carbon dioxide, and mineral salts into nourishment. This process, known as photosynthesis, is the reason such rich and diverse life exists on our planet.

But photosynthesis is a complicated process. To absorb the necessary amount of light and water, leaves must adapt to their surroundings. For example, if a plant lives in the jungle, where there is little sunlight but high humidity, it may have large leaves with a special shape that allows water to drip off quickly. In places where it's very sunny, like in the desert, leaves may shrink until they turn into spines. Many plants also have defense systems on their leaves: hairs, needles, serrated edges, and even small pits where insects can drown!

JUST LIKE ANIMALS, PLANTS ALSO BREATHE— THEY DO IT THROUGH THEIR LEAVES.

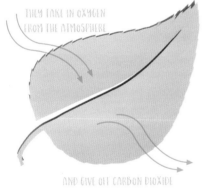

THEY TAKE IN OXYGEN FROM THE ATMOSPHERE

AND GIVE OFF CARBON DIOXIDE AND WATER VAPOR.

DURING THE DAY THEY TAKE ADVANTAGE OF THE LIGHT TO ENGAGE IN PHOTOSYNTHESIS, WHICH REVERSES THE PROCESS. LEAVES TAKE IN CARBON DIOXIDE AND THROUGH PHOTOSYNTHESIS RELEASE OXYGEN.

THE NEAR-SIGHTED ELEPHANT

Elephants are pretty special animals: their hearing, sense of smell, and memory are excellent. However, they can't see very well: since their eyes are located on the sides of their head, it's hard for them to see what's in front of them, especially if it's small. It's been thought that elephants are scared of mice. In reality, an elephant perceives something small that is moving, but can't quite make out what it is. It could be dangerous. That's why, understandably, it defends itself.

When an animal weighing 6,600 pounds (3,000 kilograms) fights for its life, it's better to keep your distance. Zookeepers say that elephants are not as gentle as they seem. They can be dangerous because you never know what they are going to do next. A blow from an elephant's trunk could kill a person.

THE TRUTH ABOUT CHOCOLATE

Many foods that are traditional in Europe, like potatoes in the northern countries and tomatoes on the Mediterranean shore, originated in the Americas, as is the case with chocolate.

This fabulous food was invented by ancient Mesoamericans as early as 1900 BCE! The Mayans and Aztecs prepared it by mashing up cacao seeds with hot spices, and they considered it a regal beverage.

Of course, the first factory to process cacao European style was founded in Switzerland at the beginning of the nineteenth century. Since then the Swiss have been regarded as the great experts on the secrets of chocolate.

LIFESAVING DOGS

For centuries, a hostel in the Swiss Alps has offered refuge to travelers crossing the Alps from Italy to Switzerland (and vice versa). In this hostel, great mountain dogs were crossbred to create the Saint Bernard. They became famous for rescuing travelers who got lost in the mountains, sometimes half-buried under the snow.

THE SAINT BERNARD IS ONE OF THE LARGEST DOG BREEDS, AND THE CHIHUAHUA, ORIGINALLY FROM MEXICO, IS ONE OF THE SMALLEST.

THE WEIGHT OF ONE SAINT BERNARD IS EQUIVALENT TO THE WEIGHT OF SIXTY CHIHUAHUAS.

WHILE THE SAINT BERNARD CAN WEIGH AROUND 200 POUNDS (90 KILOGRAMS), AN AVERAGE CHIHUAHUA WEIGHS AROUND 3½ POUNDS (1.5 KILOGRAMS).

A PAPER WORLD

Most of the paper we use is made from wood—in other words, from trees. This is one reason why the planet's forests are disappearing. Luckily, standards for responsible forest management are being implemented. For example, paper mills may be prohibited from cutting trees in certain areas to protect the habitats of the plants and animals that live there; they may be required to replace each tree that is chopped down and make sure that nearby rivers don't dry up and that the soil is not spoiled. These guidelines vary from place to place since many factors are taken into consideration, including the location of the forest, its size, and the economic needs of those who live in the area.

Let's read books and, above all, let's take care of our home: the Earth.

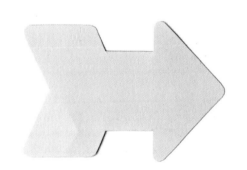